Matthew 11: 28-30
Understanding and Applying the Principle of Rest

All Rights Reserved

No part of this book may be reproduced or transmitted in any form or by any means, electronic or mechanical, including photocopying and recording or by any information storage and retrieval system without the prior written permission of the publisher except in the case of brief quotations embodied in critical articles or reviews

Unless otherwise indicated, Scripture quotations are taken from the King James Bible version of the Bible

Kamikaze for Christ Ministries
A Ministry of *Lost Sheep Ministries*
Under Pastor Bob Gibson
©2014 By Dana Poole

Table of Contents

1- Introduction   pg 5

2- Come to Rest-   Matthew 11:28   pg 11

3- Take on His Yoke-   Matthew 11:29a   pg 19

4- Learn of Him-   Matthew 11:29b   pg 25

5- Find Rest for Your Soul- Matthew 11:29c   pg 31

6- His Yoke is Easy-   Matthew 11:30   pg 37

7- The Application-   Walking in Rest   pg 43

Introduction

Before we begin to study and learn about walking in rest we must settle a matter of faith; a matter of trust in God's sovereignty. We will look at the definition of sovereignty and Scriptures that validate the sovereignty of God. Then we will allow the Holy Spirit to search our hearts and minds and reveal to us where we truly stand in this area. Do we truly believe and have unwavering faith that God is sovereign in our lives? It is so very easy to say "yes" when things are going good, but can we *truly, truly,* say that we believe it when things in life turn hard? When your heart is breaking or when your most horrific nightmare comes true? Can you really say with all boldness and confidence that God is in control? We are going to approach this topic head on and settle this matter before we move on any farther. We must do this because we cannot walk in rest if we do not believe with all our heart that the God who saved us, and delivered us is sovereign. Let's define this word *sovereign*.

Sovereignty-*supreme power or authority; independent power; unrestricted power. Sovereignty of God is His absolute right to do all things according to His own good pleasure.*

Now we will examine Scriptures concerning the sovereignty of God and let the Word speak to our hearts. Please don't read these Verses like you would the news paper, a magazine, or a recipe. This is God's Word to us concerning Himself. He wants us to understand the depths of His sovereignty because He knows that in understanding His supremacy, is where we begin to find rest. He so wants us to rest in His completed work. He desires for us to no longer struggle but to receive, trust and believe that He is above it all and has made the perfect provision for us to rest. Therefore read the following Verses as if it is the cure that you have been longer for to heal you of a terrible disease. Read these Verses like the woman with the issue of blood when she pressed through the crowd to just touch the hem of His garment. These Verses are His Hem!

Look up the following Verses in your Bible and write them out. Consider each of them very prayerfully and choose one that is speaking to your heart concerning His sovereignty.

Deuteronomy 4:39-
_____
_____
_____

1Chronicles 29:12-

Job 9:12

Psalm 29:10

Psalm 47:2

Psalm 83:18

Psalm 93:1

Daniel 2:20-22

_____
_____
_____
_____
_____
_____

Daniel 4:35

_____
_____
_____
_____

Acts 17:24-26

_____
_____
_____
_____
_____
_____
_____
_____

Which one is speaking to your heart the most? Put in your own words what that particular Verse means to you personally. Be ready to share this with the group.

_____
_____
_____
_____
_____
_____
_____

Now we must reflect on the definition and Bible verses and ask ourselves, "Why do we not rest in the sovereignty or supremacy of God?" We trust Him for our salvation, yet we don't trust Him with the day to day things that we struggle with. What keeps us from resting in Him? Why do we insist on doing things on our own? In light of those Verses my heart is proclaiming that He is more than able to all that I need Him to and more. There is no need to worry, fret or be anxious. There is nothing that is happening or can happen in my life that He is not keenly aware of and He has made a way for me to walk it out. Do you trust Him? I mean really trust Him. Can you trust Him with your broken heart, broken body or broken family? I mean the kind of trust that causes you to walk in joy no matter what is taking place around you. I mean the kind of trust that causes you to walk on the water in the middle of a stormy sea. I mean the kind of trust that gives you a grateful heart when in your life there is great lack. I mean the kind of trust that will not allow self-pity, self centeredness to rule your heart and mind. Do you have the kind of trust that, while you are in the midst of your greatest turmoil, your dive head first into the work of God and the Kingdom of God? These are all good questions but I must ask one more. Do you have the kind of trust that when things are going good you are not looking for the bottom to fall out under your feet? Now, come on, you know what I am talking about. Many of us do not rest in the easy times of our journey because we are sure something bad is going to happen, so we are constantly looking for it and guarding our selves. That is not rest. Right now, ask the Holy Spirit to speak to your heart about the areas where you are not trusting, therefore you are not resting. This must be done before you can go on. You cannot truly rest if you do not trust the one you are to rest in. Be real with yourself and with God. This could be a great turning point for you. Below Write out what is revealed to you and what you must do to correct that area of distrust. Use Scripture to back up why you can trust God and let that be your truth in that area from now on.

_____
_____
_____
_____
_____
_____
_____
_____
_____
_____
_____

Now read Psalm 139. The entire chapter. Read it several times. Don't read your footnotes in your Bible or any commentaries. Ask the Holy Spirit to show you all the areas of God's sovereignty that are represented in that one chapter. Write out here what you have come to see in that chapter.

_____
_____
_____
_____
_____
_____
_____
_____
_____
_____
_____

Now begin memorizing Matthew 11:28-30. Write it out here from your Bible

_____
_____
_____
_____
_____
_____
_____
_____

Purpose this week to trust and rest in the sovereign supremacy of Almighty God!!

Come to Rest

Jesus Said...........

Come unto me, all ye that labour and are heavy laden, and I will give you rest. Matthew 11:28

I love these words that Jesus spoke to us;"Come unto me........" It is so comforting, so assuring to know that He desires us to come to Him. What a privilege and honor that the King of Kings and Lord of Lords wants us to come to Him. He wants us near Him, not to lord over us as an unrighteous task master but to bless, encourage and strengthen us as a loving Savior. He knows we are most days, in over our heads. He knows our every weakness yet He loves us and desires to use us mightily for His kingdom. He chose each one of us knowing full well how much we would need Him and that He would indeed be doing all the work, especially the tough stuff. I love that about our Lord. Just think about how many times in the Bible God is reaching out to inform us that we cannot do it without Him, we are not required to do it on our own and that we can do all things through Him. Stop right now and find one Verse, **(not Philippians 4:13)** that speaks that message.

Write it out here:

_____
_____
_____

Do not be so quick to assume that you know you cannot do it alone. I think by the end of this lesson, by the help of the Holy Spirit you will learn that there are areas where you are trying to do it on your own, you just did not realize it. I pray that we all see why we are weary, and come to a clear understanding of what we must do to truly rest; to walk in rest.
Now we will begin looking at Matthew 11:28. There is a lot for us to understand about the word "come". The grammar that is used there is very significant and speaks volumes about what was going on with Jesus at that moment when He spoke those words" Come unto me". Let's take a look. According to the Greek Lexicon the word "Come" is defined as:

deuteit- is an adverb, an interjection and is derived from the root word deuro which is an imperative. Meaning "Come quick", or "Come over here" with excitement!

Now putting all that grammar and definition together we can clearly see that Jesus is not simply telling us to come to Him. He is saying with great command and excitement that we should stop whatever we are doing and come to Him quickly. Based on these definitions it's easy to imagine He must have been on His feet proclaiming to the people." Come here, come to me right now. I have great rest for your weary soul. I have the sweetest most complete rest for you, right now. Do not hesitate! Do not meander to me as if you are not sure or don't trust me. Come on, I have what you need!"

We also must look at the fact that Christ is commanding us to come. He is not simply asking, requesting or letting us know if we need rest, He's got it. It is not an invitation; it is a command. Now when Jesus, the King of Kings gives a command and we do not listen or obey, then we have entered into disobedience. If we are hanging back, half heartedly meandering to Him, or not coming to Him at all we are choosing to live in a state of disobedience. But not only that, we are robbing ourselves of rest and allowing weariness, heaviness and work to control us or manipulate our mind, will and emotions. Jesus has the perfect way to free us from all of that and put us in a place of rest and victory. Hallelujah!!

So what is our problem? I asked the Lord the same thing. I asked Him, why is it that we think we are coming to Him but in actuality we are not because we are still so very weary and heavy laden. This is what He has shown me. So often we come to Him with our problem, issues, hurts, weakness, illness and talk to Him about them like we talk to someone on the phone. We tell Him all about it, how it pains us so and weighs us down, but do we stop and let Him speak to us about it? Do we search His Word and let the power of the Word set our heart and mind straight about what is keeping us from resting? We spend too much time telling Him or others our perspective on things instead of seeking God's perspective on it. Too often we assume that God sees things the same way we do. I have found more often that He does not. We must come to Him with a completely open heart, with trust in Him and His faithfulness. We must come to Him willing to change our hearts and minds even if we don't understand or like it. We must come to Him through His Word forsaking our own way and conforming to His.

There are many ways that we come to Him. But first and foremost, we must come to Him in faith. Faith in who He is, what He has done and in expectation of what He will do; then and only then are we truly coming to Him.

What is your favorite "faith" Verse? Why does that Verse encourage your faith? Write it out in the space provided

_____
_____
_____
_____

There are 3 major avenues that we can come to Him.

<u>Prayer</u>
We should be cultivating a very intimate prayer walk with our Lord. One that is equal in listening as well as speaking. It is in the times when we wait and listen that our hearts and minds are changed by that still small voice of our Savior. It is then that we begin to come to Him for that rest our soul desires.

<u>The Word</u>
It is vital to our well being to have a close relationship with the Word of God. We can come to Him through seeking Him in the Word of God; those quiet alone times with just you and the Word can be the most powerful. It is then that we know the heart of God on our situation and can gain the trust and confidence that causes us to rest in His Word.

<u>Other believers</u>
When we fellowship with other believers by coming to church, being taught the Word, or being used to bless others, we are coming to Him. We are surrounding ourselves with HIS people, HIS purpose, and HIS kingdom. When we disconnect from the church or other believers we cannot say that we are coming to Him. If we are truly coming to Him then we should be involved in everything He is involved in.

If we are not coming to Him in all of the above ways then there is a disconnection on our part, not His. We must set our priorities and come to Him in all the avenues possible to us. If we are not then we are still doing it our own way, and we are still very tired, weary and worn out. When we come to Him we must bring it all. Bring our hearts, our mind, our will and emotions. We must give up our right to be hurt, or angry or tired. We must give up striving to overcome on our own. We must give up our own strength and our own way of handling things. We must give up self-pity and self-centeredness. We have no right to feel sorry for ourselves. I know that is hard to hear, but feeling sorry for ourselves keeps us in bondage to pain, hurt, illness, or whatever has lead us to the place of self-pity. Sometimes we take up a weird sort of pride about our struggle because when others feel sorry for us it brings us comfort; or when others tell us how strong we are we may begin to celebrate our hurt or struggle. But that sort of comfort is a lie and only promotes and comforts self. It is a trick of the enemy and is designed to keep us from entering into the rest that God has provided for us. When we come to Him we must come with the attitude that we are letting go of it all; the good, bad and the ugly. We must come with our whole being. We must give up our right to be weary. I am not being overly harsh or negative; I know this to be truth. I have MS and have had it for 25 years. I deal with bouts of overwhelming fatigue. During one of my times of prayer as I cried out to the Lord at the start of my day, He spoke that to me. I must give up my right to be tired or He cannot raise me above the weariness that I was experiencing every day of my life. If we think we have a right to feel sorry for ourselves or to be tired and worn out then He will let us have that right and that weariness and hurt will continue to be with us. I have changed how I come to Him and have experienced more victory over this struggle in my life. Not because of my strength but because He raises me above it all and takes me past my limitations. I get more done in a day and I do it with great joy and peace, not a struggle.

We must get to a place where we are willing to let all of it go so when we come to Him we are able to receive the strength that we need to walk in such a way that glorifies Him, not glorifies our struggle. Do we go through times where we are dealing with hurts, and sorting through anger, emotions, and questions? Yes we do and there is no condemnation in that but we cannot stay there. We must come to Him and begin letting it go and rising above it. Do we get physically tired and need to rest? Oh yes we do, Christ did and He rested. But when we find that our physical state, whether it be sickness, or fatigue, determines what we do, or keeps us from any of those avenues of coming to Him then we are not letting Him have those areas. Our bodies should not be controlling us, demanding its own way or keeping us from our Lord. Let me state here that this is not an area where we should be legalistic and it is an individual thing between you and the Lord. He alone is your Judge.

Now let's look at the rest of the Verse. Matthew 11:28. Come unto me all ye that *labour* and are heavy *laden* and I will give you rest.
We will look at the 2 items Christ listed that is the cause of our weariness.
According to the Greek Lexicon the word "labour" and "laden" is defined as:

Labour- Kapiao- verb, meaning to grow weary, tired, exhausted with toils, burdens or grief.
Laden-Phortizo- verb, meaning to load, to load one with a burden of rites and unwarranted precepts

Look at those definitions and rejoice, because Christ knows exactly what is weighing us down. We are carrying burdens and grief, which cause us to be weary and tired. He knows it makes us physically exhausted. He sees the heaviness of us trying hard to be righteous, to be good, and to be Christ like. He sees that we are laden with the wrong thinking of, I have to do good works! As Christ is bidding us to come to Him He sees the heaviness of all we carry. I am sure it breaks His heart to see it on us when He has done all that is necessary for us to not be weighed down. The Bible tells us in 6 different Verses in the Gospels what Christ thinks we need to do to have freedom from the struggles of this life. Look up the following Verses in your Bible. Matthew 10:39, Matthew 16:25, Mark 8:35, Luke 9:24, Luke 17:33, John 12:25. I prefer the one in John the most, it speaks directly to my heart. We are to lose our life in Him in order to find REAL life! Life with purpose, with eternal purposes! Now look up the next set of Verses, 1Corinthians 6:20, 1Corinthians 7:23, 1Corinthians 6:19.
Who do we belong to and how did that come to be?

_____

_____

Really think about this if we put together what Christ is telling us in those 6 Verses from the Gospels and what Paul is telling us in those Verses in 1Corinthians what must we do?

_____

_____

_____

In your opinion do you think if you practiced those Biblical principles you would be free from the labor and heavy laden burdens that this life would heap upon you ? If yes is your answer explain why. If no is your answer explain why.

_____
_____
_____
_____
_____
_____

Now let's look at the word rest from the Greek Lexicon

Rest- Anapauo- verb To cause or permit one to cease from any movement or labor in order to recover or collect ones strength. To refresh. To keep quiet or calm and patient with expectation.

Wow, I don't know about you but I have spent most of my walk with the Lord , NOT resting. I think the part of that definition that convicts my heart the most is the calm and patient expectation. We can never have this kind of rest while we are living our life for ourselves, holding on to things we think we have a right to, and not truly recognizing that we have been bought with a price, a very precious price. I am truly humbled by what the Word has revealed to me. I am determined and desperate to enter that rest everyday and stay in it. There is too much that I purpose to do for the Kingdom and I must not let weariness keep me from it any longer. I have no right to tiredness. I must consider Hebrews 12:3-4 *For consider him that endured such contradiction of sinners against himself, lest ye be wearied and faint in your minds. Ye have not yet resisted unto blood, striving against sin.*

Not one of us has suffered as much as our Savior. Nor have been as hurt or as heartbroken as He was on the cross that day. He endured so we did not have to carry the heaviness of all the iniquity that can befall us as we walk in this world. Yet we cling to it anyway.

Right Now ask the Holy Spirit to show you what you are holding back when you come to Him. What is the source of your weariness? What is it that you have claimed rights to? Are you not coming to Him in one of the areas that is available to you? Be totally honest with yourself and allow time for the Holy Spirit to speak with you. Write out what is revealed to you and find Scripture to confirm it. Also write out your plan of action to correct it. This is completely private and will not be required to share in the group.

_____
_____
_____
_____
_____
_____
_____
_____
_____
_____
_____
_____
_____
_____
_____
_____
_____
_____
_____
_____
_____
_____
_____
_____
_____

Continue memorizing Matthew 11:28-30 write it out 5 times.

1
___

2
___

3
___

4
___

5
___

Take on His Yoke

Jesus Said.........

      Take my yoke upon you............. Matthew 11:29a

Christ is telling us here that He has a yoke. The yoke that Christ wore is not one of bondage it is one of submission to authority. Let's look at the definition from the Greek Lexicon.

Yoke- zü-go's, serving to couple two things together is used metaphorically to show submission to authority.

How beautiful Christ's example of submission to the Father! Before we talk about what this yoke means to us, we must look at the yoke that Christ wore while He was here. I want to encourage you to approach this subject fresh and to not lean on any past teaching you may have had. For example, "yoke up with Jesus and your load will not be so heavy". That statement is a truth however Christ is saying so much more than that as He is making this statement to the people. I asked the Lord to show me in His Word where we can see the Yoke that Christ wore. As we go through the Verses keep in mind the definition of the yoke that is listed above.

Write out the following Verses and explain in your own words how it shows Christ wearing the yoke of submission to authority, His Father's authority. I want to encourage you to not look up commentaries or depend on any foot notes in your Bible. Look up the Verses in different Bible translations or look up definitions, BUT most of all ask the Holy Spirit to show you what He wants you to see and be patient. Make time to ponder and mediate until you receive a clear understanding. You will be surprised at what He will show you!!

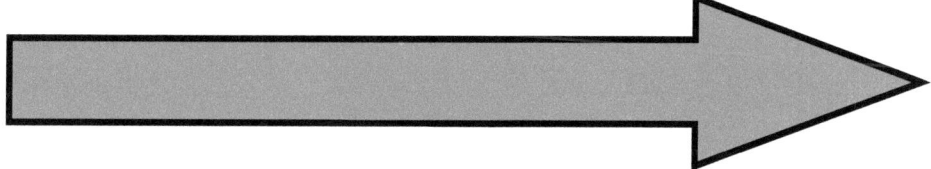

John 5:19

___

John 5:30

___

John 6:38

___

Matthew 26: 39,42

___

Hebrews 5:8

___

John 4:4-34 *(you do not have to write this one out) REALLY take some time with this one! Look for all the ways it shows Christ submission to the Father. What was the end result of His obedience and who was it for?*

___

I love the fact that the Word of God gives us such a clear account of Christ's example of submission to the authority of His Father. What we need to take from this, is that as Christ is instructing us to take on His yoke He is telling us, if you want *real* rest, then it begins with complete submission to the authority of God in EVERY area of our lives. Not just the big areas, but the little ones as well. Before we get introspective we need to go to the Word of God and let it speak to our hearts about submission and rest. Keep in mind that these Verses may not use the word submission but instead use humble, it is the same concept.

Please follow the same instructions as before concerning foot notes and commentaries. Explain in your own words how each Verse is instructing you on submission and what the rest or blessing that comes from doing so. Take time and mediate on the Verses and how they apply to your life. (you do not have to write out these Verses.)

Philippians 2:5-9

Psalm 10:17

1 Peter 5:5-7

James 4:7

James 4:10

1 Peter 2:12-14
_____
_____
_____
_____

Matthew 23:12
_____
_____
_____
_____

Christ is showing us by His example and proving to us in His Word that if we submit to the Supreme Authority of God we will find that true rest that we long for, which we desperately need. I have been so challenged by the Holy Spirit to be brave and allow Him to look at ALL the aspects of my life. The active times and inactive times; my life of service and work; and my life of leisure and fun. What areas I still claim for myself and what I have given to Him. Who I spend my time with and how I spend my time. What types of conversations I have and what words do I use. Who and what I value and if I allow it to keep me from coming to God in all the ways available to me. My motives for what I do whether it be obligation or obedience to what I am called to do. God does not intend us to pick at ourselves constantly questioning ourselves; He simply wants us to allow the Holy Spirit to show us what He wants us to see. Our Lord loves us so very much and has done all that is needed for us to walk in complete rest each moment of everyday. He wants to make your "to do" list, set your agenda for each day because He alone knows what lies ahead. He alone sets the requirements for us each day. We must give up ALL control. We must submit to His authority, follow Christ's example and humble ourselves to the instruction of His Word. Everyday can truly be an adventure when we let HIS will be done each day and stop acting and planning our day independently from Him. You may say, "I ask the Lord everyday to order my steps" but I challenge you to really look long and hard at what you do with your time every day. Are you serving yourself, your home, your own life or are you participating in KINGDOM work. Does Kingdom work fit into your schedule only if nothing else comes up? For those of us in full time ministry I ask this question; are you serving the Kingdom or are you a slave to obligations? I challenge you to take notice of what you do and ask the Holy Spirit to reveal to you your motives. Can you be brave? Can you not reason things away with justifications? Can you be completely honest with yourself? Please keep in mind that this is one more step closer to experiencing that true rest. Be determined to not allow anything to keep you from the rest that is promised you. Stop Right now and pray. Give the Holy Spirit permission to search your heart. *On the next page write out anything and everything that is revealed to you. This may take more than one day. Purpose to keep your mind and heart focused on listening to the Holy Spirit. This is not a time to hunt down everything you do wrong. God knows what you need to see and change.*

Jesus Said..........

    Take my yoke upon you.............. Matthew 11:29a

Continue memorizing Matthew 11:28-30 write it out 5 times.

1 _____
_____
_____
_____

2 _____
_____
_____
_____

3 _____
_____
_____
_____

4 _____
_____
_____
_____

5 _____
_____
_____
_____

Learn of Him

Jesus Said.........
Learn of me; for I am meek and lowly of heart
Matthew 11:29b

Christ is telling us here to look at what He does and how He does it and duplicate it. How comforting it is that we do not have to figure out how to rest, however I think that is what I have been doing up until now. It is very clear to me by just looking up the Words that Christ used to express this to us, that I have been missing it for way too long. But praise be to God He did not let me strive on my own too long and brought me to this precious passage of Scripture that has liberated me. One thing that has always intrigued me when I read about the life of Christ is the simplicity of His life. I have always wanted that same simplicity and through study these Verses He has shown me the way. Let's begin by clearly defining a few words.

The first thing Christ says is "Learn of me", we will see what the transliteration is from the Greek Lexicon

Learn-*manthano*-verb
To be apprised, to increase one's knowledge, to hear, to be informed, to learn by use or practice, to be in the habit of, accustomed to

Vines Expository –
To be learning "Christ" is not simply the doctrine of Christ, but Christ Himself, a process not merely getting to know the person but of applying the knowledge as to walk differently from the rest of the Gentiles, Ephesians 4:20

These definitions describe a person who is not simply gathering information about Christ, but a person who is taking what they know and walking in it. This person is a follower of Christ, a true disciple; they are not just studying the Word for intellectual pursuit, but for their own life. An individual who is responding to Christ's command to "learn of me" is allowing the Word of God to transform their character into the image of Christ. We must move on and define exactly how Christ describes Himself. He says He is MEEK and LOWLY

Greek Lexicon
Meek- Praos adjective
Gentle, mild, mildness of disposition, gentleness of spirit
This Greek word appears only 1 time in the New Testament
Lowly-
of low degree, humble, base, cast down, of low estate, lowly.
This Greek Word is translated from the KJV 7 more times.

We will look up these Verses and let the Word of God bring a very clear understanding to our heart. Look them up and write them out.

Luke 1:52
_____
_____
_____
_____

Romans 12:16
_____
_____
_____
_____

2 Corinthians 7:6
_____
_____
_____

2 Corinthians 10:1
_____
_____
_____
_____

James 1:9
_____
_____
_____
_____

James 4:6
_____
_____
_____
_____

1 Peter 5:5
_____
_____
_____
_____

We must not dismiss that Christ said He is meek and lowly in **heart**. Let's define heart.
Greek Lexicon
Heart-Kardia-noun
the center and seat of spiritual life
the soul or mind, as it is the fountain and seat of the thoughts, passions, desires, appetites, affections, purposes, endeavors
of the understanding, the faculty and seat of the intelligence
of the will and character of the soul so far as it is affected and stirred in a bad way or good, or of the soul as the seat of the sensibilities, affections, emotions, desires, appetites, passions

When I ponder on the definition of heart it becomes very real to me that Christ is not telling us to act or behave meek and lowly He is telling us to **become** meek and lowly. I don't know about you but that's pretty hard to do. I do not have a meek and lowly switch that I can just turn on and I am sure neither do you. So what then are we to do when it is very clear that He is telling us this is the heart attitude we must have? So I asked the Lord this question. *"Lord how am I to walk in this great rest you have for me if it depends on my heart being meek and lowly, because I am so far from that. Am I destined to be weary because I cannot attain this state of humility that is required?"* He so sweetly led me back to the first part of this Verse when He said that we are to take on His yoke. You see it's not our yoke, it's not the preachers yoke, it is Christ's yoke and in that yoke is HIS meekness and HIS lowliness of heart and it becomes ours! It becomes what drives our passions, appetites and desires just as it did Christ. When we say yes to His yoke His character becomes ours. We will have a heart like His. This is a process of transformation that we go through and will never stop going through until we see Him face to face. The important thing is to stay in process. Study Him and His Word and follow it, apply it, conform to it. Seek understanding from the Holy Spirit. When you find that you are heavy laden, weary and worn out you must check your heart attitude. Ask yourself if you have taken on Christ's yoke? Have you positioned yourself under the authority of God just as Christ did? Have you yielded all control to Him? Who is making your "to do" list every day? How do you handle interruptions in your day by people and circumstances? As you walk out each day pay close attention to your own thoughts, actions and reactions, bring them captive and tell yourself that you have taken on Christ's yoke and you are walking in His meekness and lowliness. You are at rest in all that He has done for you! It is His character that you walk in! Hallelujah!

Take your time with the homework questions and be sure to work on your memorization of Matthew 11:28-30. We are half way through and God has so much more for us to come to know. I am sure that as we press in to these truths and ask Him to help us in our yielding and trusting, He will be there with His grace to see us through and to do in us what we cannot do ourselves.

Based on the definitions and the Verses on meekness and lowliness how would you describe a person that is meek and lowly? How would they interact with people? How would you know they were meek and lowly?

_____
_____
_____

Which one of those Verses speaks to you the most? Write it out here and be ready to share with the group.

_____
_____
_____

According to the lesson what is the difference between trying to **act** or **behave** meek and **being** meek?

_____
_____
_____

Read the following Verses: Galatians 5:22-25, 2 Corinthians 4:7, Romans 8:9-11. How do these Verses confirm for us that Christ's meekness and lowliness can be manifested in and through us?

_____
_____
_____

Considering the previous question, we see that it is His meekness however according to this lesson what must we do to be partakers of this wonderful rest that Christ is talking to us about? (hint it is in the Verse for this lesson)

_____
_____
_____

What are some ways that we can and should be actively "learning of Him"?

_____
_____

What keeps us from doing those things?
___
___

What will you do in your life to assure you are actively "learning of Him" continually?
___
___
___

What will hinder Christ's meekness and lowliness from being manifested in our lives?
___
___
___

Why do you think Christ instructed us to, *"take my yoke upon you and learn of me, for I am meek and lowly of heart"*, as a prerequisite to rest?
___
___
___
___
___

On this page write out a prayer to the Lord telling Him your desire to learn of Him and how you purpose to allow His meekness and lowliness to manifest in and through you.
___
___
___
___
___
___
___
___
___
___
___
___
___
___
___
___

Continue memorizing Matthew 11:28-30 write it out 5 times.

1

2

3

4

5

Find Rest for Your Soul

Jesus Said.........
> And ye shall find rest for your souls.
> Matthew 11:29c

This lesson is by far my favorite. This is where we put together everything that we have been studying and meditating on. I can see the heart of Christ so plainly as I have written these lessons. He is so urgently calling us to this place of rest. He knows that He alone has what we need. He is exclaiming with excitement that we come to Him. He sees the labor and heavy loads that we carry. He is commanding us as our King to come to Him because He knows we are needlessly carrying those loads and our labor is in our own limited strength. That is pure love that is speaking those words, "Come unto me"! How beautiful. The King of Glory bids me come! The Lord of all is watching ever so carefully over my life and by His grace and compassion calls me to Himself when I am loaded up with burdens too great for me. Then He so sweetly begins to instruct me how to enter the rest He has for me. It truly is very simple. To put Verse 29 all together, He is simply telling us,

"Let me have control because you don't really know what needs to be done each day. Let me guide you because you can trust me. Everything will be according to God's perfect will. Let my meek and lowly character bring soundness to your heart and mind that you not worry and fret."

When we allow the meekness of Christ to rule us, we have no agenda of our own, only to do the will of God; and if that is our motive then God moves in a mighty way and His almighty strength is manifested in us and through us. We will find that we accomplish so much more. That we are resting as we walk or as we serve. Because we are women everything is service. When we clean our homes, cook, go shopping for groceries and all those chores, we are serving our families. God desires that we rest in Him as we do every little thing. We have the Creator of the universe wanting to strengthen **while** we do the Laundry!! WOW now that's amazing. He wants us to rest and simply be the vehicle for His power!

When we take on His yoke of submission we position ourselves to rest in His power; we find rest. This lesson is dealing with the part of the Verse that tells us what we find in that rest. We find rest for our souls. Our soul is made up of our mind, will and emotions. Our minds are like very complex computers and never turn off, even when we are sleeping. Everything begins and ends with the mind. Our will is what drives us and it is our "decider". Our emotions, (well as women we are pretty aware of these) are where we feel and where our passions operate. Now let me take a side step here for a moment and talk about our emotions. God gave us all emotions men and women. Emotions are not bad. They are not signs of weakness. However to be controlled by them is very dangerous because most our emotional responses are temporary and will change frequently. To be unemotional is not good and does not demonstrate strength, in fact it actually is the contrary. To feel them and not know you have the freedom to express them is a sad place to be and is actually a type of bondage. Men typically have this issue and I think it is because society has labeled emotions as signs of weakness. But God says we are created in His image, He gave us emotions, and therefore they are good! Our emotions are part of our soul and when our soul is being controlled by the Holy Spirit it is a beautiful thing! God will use our emotions to reveal to us how He feels about something. With the experience of our emotions is where we find what we are passionate about and it is where we find that deep, desperate need for God. Through our emotions is where the fervent righteous prayer comes from. We must be ever so careful with these emotions because if they get out of submission to the Holy Spirit, they will lie to you and get you to believing things that are not true and making decisions based on "feelings" instead of truth. It is a very fine line and balance is achieved only through our intimate relationship with God and yielding to the Holy Spirit. Ok now back to finding rest for our souls. When we enter that place of trust, yielding, and submitting we find sweet rest for our minds, our will and our emotions. Just think about it. If those three areas are at rest then we are REALLY resting. What does a mind that is at rest look like? How does it function? Look up the following Scriptures. Explain in your own words how they each speak of a mind at rest.

Philippians 4:6-7

_____
_____
_____
_____
_____

Romans 8:6

_____
_____
_____

Philippians 2:5

_____
_____
_____

According to the lesson how do we enter into this rest for our minds?

_____
_____
_____
_____

If our minds are at rest, then our will and emotions will be also. It all starts in our mind. Our minds must be able to tell our will and emotions that we can trust truth; that we can trust our Lord. It is so very crucial to our entire beings that we enter this rest. A mind that is not resting is one that is thinking, thinking, thinking, and thinking. Trying to figure things out. It will be thinking phrases, like "but, what if", "I don't understand", " why, why, why" or "this doesn't make sense" Attached to all of those phrases are a mixture of emotions like strife, worry, anxiety, stress and torment. While that is going on with your mind and emotions your will is scrambling trying to decide what you are going to do, how to react to something or someone. Your will is desperately trying to figure out what direction to move you in. It wants to make a decision and move you in that direction. I searched the Word of God for places where He addressed our emotions and I really did not find one. I also looked for Scriptures where He talked with us about our will, but I only found Verses that addressed Christ surrendering His will to the Lord, or Verses about the Will of God. I only found Verses that instruct us about our minds, as I had you look up already. Therefore, I am very confident in stating this fact: Our will and emotions are purely motivated by what we think. That is why it is crucial that we are constantly in the Word. Look up Romans 12:1-2 write it out here:

_____
_____
_____
_____

We must have a very close relationship with the Word of God, which transforms our thoughts to think like God. That it moves us to go to Him, trust His supremacy, take on His yoke and find that sweet rest for our minds that calms and settles our will and brings balance to our emotions.

In your own words describe what it is like to have a soul that has entered the rest described in this lesson.

_____
_____
_____

What are your "symptoms" when you are not resting?

_____
_____
_____

What should you do if you find those symptoms in your life?

_____
_____
_____
_____

Think of a time in your life, could be now, could have been in the past, where you would have handled a situation differently if you had been resting. Describe it and explain what you would do differently.

_____
_____
_____
_____
_____
_____

In your opinion how strongly does God feel about us walking in this rest and why. Use Scripture to validate your answer. Be ready to share your answer with the group.

_____
_____
_____
_____
_____
_____

What will you do from now on when you find yourself in a place of turmoil and unrest?

_____
_____
_____
_____

If you were to counsel someone about walking in rest what would you say and how would you pray for them. Be very specific and use at least 2 different Scriptures. (if you use Matthew 11:28-30 it only counts as one Verse)

_____
_____
_____
_____
_____
_____
_____
_____

How important is it to you to walk in this rest? Why?

_____
_____
_____
_____
_____
_____
_____
_____

How can walking in rest effect the relationship with your family, friends or coworkers?

_____
_____
_____
_____

Referring to the italicized statement on the first page of this lesson; how does that statement effect you?

_____
_____
_____
_____

Make a list of things that normally stress you out or you worry about them:

_____   _____
_____   _____
_____   _____

Now Right out a statement or proclamation that you give Christ control and you purpose to rest and not stress or worry!

_____
_____
_____
_____
_____
_____

Continue memorizing Matthew 11:28-30 write it out 5 times.

1. _____
_____
_____
_____

2. _____
_____
_____
_____

3. _____
_____
_____
_____

4. _____
_____
_____
_____

5. _____
_____
_____
_____

His Yoke is Easy

Jesus Said.........

For my yoke is easy and my burden is light
Matthew 11:30

Christ's yoke and burden was simply to do the Will of God every moment He was here. In all of His 33 years everything He did was what God wanted Him to do. It was all for us and according to God's plan of redemption for you and me. Christ's entire existence was for us. He never did anything for Himself and always pointed others to the Father. He is our example. Once we are born again we have been made ministers of reconciliation. We have a great purpose and a plan for our existence as well. Our purpose is to do the will of God, and point others to Jesus, who is the instrument of reconciliation. His yoke is so very easy because He has already done all the work for us. Moses brought us the Law and Christ fulfilled it for all of mankind because we could never be good enough. Quit trying to be good enough and rest under the yoke of Christ! His burden is easy. What is required of us as we are under His yoke? Live, to live a joyful and victorious life. Will things always be easy? Oh no, BUT under His yoke of grace the burden of all the cares of this world and this life are merely tools to grow us and prove His strength and love. I think where we miss it is in 2 main areas.

#1- We are still trying to be good. We are still trying to please God and make Him happy as if He is upset with us.
#2- We think that His yoke is hard, no fun, or maybe we think that our purpose is works and servitude. We feel obligatory to serve instead of having passion to serve; therefore there is no joy, only drudgery.

This lesson will address these 2 points. I know there is much more that we can go into however, as I prayed about this lesson these are the 2 points that the Holy Spirit keeps bringing to me, therefore we will dig into this. We will search the Word of God and seek His heart. I know He wants His children resting in the completed work of Christ.

To begin addressing point #1 we will we start in Hebrews 4:1-11. How many times is the word REST mentioned in those 11 Verses? _____. That is quite a bit. Now read those 11 verses again.

The rest that is being referred to is our eternal rest in Heaven as well as the rest we have access to now through faith. This rest is not about us being good enough, righteous or how much we do for Him. We enter this rest by faith and only by faith. In fact it is not about us at all. It is about what Christ did for us. When we are resting and walking in that rest we glorify Him and bless Him; for that is what He came to do for us. His yoke is one of submission yes, but it is also one of grace. We must submit to the fact that what we have done in the past is irrelevant to our resting. We confess our sins to our loving God and He wipes it away!! There is nothing more for us to do. Matthew Henry says this about Verse 10-

"Every true believer hath ceased from his own works of righteousness, and from the burdensome works of the law, as God and Christ have ceased from their works of creation and redemption."

We must receive by faith the completed work of redemption by Christ and thank Him each day for His yoke of grace. Declare to Him that you submit to His work on the cross therefore you cease your own works! Rest in what He has done for you beloved!

Prayerfully answer the following questions:

Why do we still try to be good enough?

_____
_____
_____

What is the difference between trying to be good enough and trying to do what's right in the eyes of God?

_____
_____
_____

As a believer why are you already good enough? Use Scripture to validate your answer

_____
_____
_____
_____

According to Hebrews 4:11, we are to be laboring to enter the rest that is promised us, therefore because labor is something you do, what are some things that we can do that will help us enter that rest?

_____
_____
_____
_____

Now we will address point #2.
We will begin by defining the Word obligation:

An act or course of action to which a person is morally or legally bound; a duty or commitment;

God does not want us to serve Him out of obligation. He is not holding us legally obligated to anything. He does not want to be an obligation, or duty that we must perform. Christ came, fulfilled the law and set us free from the condemnation of the law and the bondage of it.. God desires us to serve Him from a deep seeded passion that we have for Him. He desires that we find the passion He has placed in us and let that be the driving force that causes us to serve. Now we will define passion:

A strong feeling of enthusiasm or excitement for something or about doing something.

That touches my heart and changes my perspective about serving. He wants us to have enthusiasm, excitement about serving Him. When we function from the area of passion, there is joy; there is peace, even when it is hard you find that you have in you what it takes to do what is needed to do. God never intended us to be men pleasers or slaves to obligations. Look up Ephesians 6:5-7, Colossians 3:22-23, Romans 7:6. After reading the Verses what do you think God is telling us about serving Him; what should our heart attitude be?

_____
_____
_____
_____

According to the definitions of obligation and passion, what is the difference between them?

_____
_____
_____

Now consider this passage for the Message Bible about Caleb:
Numbers 14:24 the Message
"But my servant Caleb—this is a different story. He has a different spirit; he follows me passionately. I'll bring him into the land that he scouted and his children will inherit it."

What did God say about Caleb and how is God blessing Caleb?

_____
_____
_____

We must never forget that Christ is our example and He endured extreme hardship; hardships that we truly no nothing about. He was given the grace, strength and power to endure because He surrendered all control, all leadership, to the Father. He had no agenda of His own. Every minute of the day was planned by Father God. He endured the Cross by giving up His will and surrendering to the Will of His Father. Luke 22:42-

*Saying, Father, if thou be willing, remove this cup from me: nevertheless **not my will**, but thine, be done.*

Do we live our lives like that? Do we truly let Him have control in every area or do we make our "to-do" list every day? Do we let how we feel dictate what we do? Do we think it doesn't matter; do we think He is not interested in the small things? Are we functioning according to obligation or passion? Are we working and serving based on needs or based on what the Spirit of God is telling us? Are we serving people or God? Only you and the Lord can answer these questions. But they need to be answered before you move on to the last lesson.

Let the Holy Spirit examine your heart. Ask Him to reveal to you the answers to all those questions. Write down what He shows you. Try not to be too general. Be very specific and detailed here.

_____
_____
_____
_____
_____
_____
_____
_____
_____
_____
_____
_____
_____
_____
_____
_____
_____

Continue memorizing Matthew 11:28-30 write it out 5 times.

1
___

2
___

3
___

4
___

5
___

The Application

Jesus Said.........

Come unto me, all ye that labour and are heavy laden and I will give you rest. Take my yoke upon you, and learn of me; for I am meek and lowly in heart: and ye shall find rest unto your souls. For my yoke is easy, and my burden is light.

Matthew 11:28-30

This lesson is where the rubber meets the road. All of the knowledge and understanding that we have been gaining means nothing if we do not apply it. We can define all kinds of words, translate them from the Greek and Hebrew, outline great Biblical principles, and write wonderful Bible studies, if it is not applied, it truly means nothing. I have been pressing in on this topic for many years. Seeking the Lord on it and asking the Holy Spirit to teach me, however it's only been in the last few months that I have really studied the Word concerning resting. What I have given you in the previous 6 lessons is information and you have been challenged to be introspective. If you have allowed the Holy Spirit to search you and you have been honest with yourself then you are ready for the application. It begins with prayer. It begins with making a mental, emotional, and spiritual choice to allow Him to have complete control of the present day. Many times throughout this Bible study I spoke about your "to-do" list. We all have them whether they are written down or in our minds. If we are going to walk in rest then we have to **stop** making our own "to-do" list and then asking Him to bless it and help us to finish it. We need to allow Him to lead us and if we need a list we must let Him make it. We need to come to Him at the beginning of the day recognizing that we need His guidance, we need Him to be in control. You have to begin your day resting. Too often we go and go in our own strength and then cry out for help when we think we have reached the end of ourselves. However, what we must realize is at the start of each day we are at the end of ourselves. We need Him. We must come to Him and begin our day resting in His sovereignty, trusting that He is in control. Then we must bring it all; the good, bad and ugly. Hold nothing back. We must declare to Him that we are taking on His yoke of submission and authority; following His example of meekness and humility, seeking the will of God for that day. We must forsake our own agenda and search our own hearts for areas where self or the flesh is ruling. Thank Him for the ease of His yoke and the lightness of His burden because He did all the work for you. The following is an example how I apply this principle at the start of my day.

My God how thankful I am that you are sovereign and supreme, over all things. Thank You that I can safely trust You with all of me today. You are always faithful! Thank you that I need not fret or be anxious concerning this day. I come to You my Lord, obeying Your command to come. I thank You that you have rest for me; true rest for me to walk in this day. I eagerly come to You with every care and concern that troubles my heart and I give them to You. I purpose to not allow those things to keep me from resting, because when I rest, I glorify You and bless others that I come in contact with. I need strength and energy today from You; my own is not sufficient. Convict me when I am striving on my own and not coming to You through all the avenues that You have provided. Lord, I take on Your yoke of submission and humility and I purpose to follow your example of meekness today. I say to You my Lord, not my will but Yours be done. I give You all control to lead me and guide my every step. Show me what I am to do today and help me to hear Your voice all throughout the day as you prompt me to the left and to the right. I have no agenda of my own and You alone know what is needful for me to do every minute of this day. Create in me a heart like Yours that obeys the Father, loves others and is selfless. I thank You for the rest that giving you control brings me. I praise You for the balance that you bring my soul and that I truly rest in that perfectness. For your yoke of grace is easy and Your burden is light because the work is already been done for me on the cross. I do cease from my own works this day and thank you right now for all I will accomplish for Your glory and honor today. Thank You Lord, I am walking in rest today!

This is just an example of what my prayer life has been like the last few months. It has been amazing. I get more done and as I am working I am at peace. I am not stressed. I am slowly identifying all the things in my life that are obligations to people, that God did not call me to do. I am finding that what I think needs to be done is not always what God wants me to do. I hear Him speak to me and lead me in what I should do; He even reminds me of things I have forgotten. I find myself saying, "I forgot" a whole lot less. The more and more I take all the things I have learned from Matthew 11:28-30 and apply them to my prayer life, the easier things are, the more I get done and I am at peace when I lay my head on my pillow. The key is to listen for Him throughout your day and allow Him to make changes to your day and reveal things to you that He wants you to know. If I get frustrated or overwhelmed I simply remind myself that I am under His yoke, He is in control and His yoke is easy; because I truly know what that means now, it causes a rest to come over me and the negative emotions wash away as His rest consumes me. Many times He shows me that I am allowing needs to pull me around; whether it is needs of others or just stuff that needs to be done. I am to be led by Him, every need that presents itself is not my responsibility to meet. Sometimes I need to say NO to people and it is ok to do that. I can rest in that! I allow Him to interrupt my day and I have learned to rest in that. When someone comes in the church office and needs my attention for a few minutes I give it quickly because people are important. He will make it all work out, somehow I will get everything done, He is in control. Hallelujah!

I have found that it helps me to really retain something I have been taught if I share it with someone. So this week, share the entire Bible study with someone. Covering all 6 lessons and write out how they responded.

_____
_____
_____
_____
_____

What part of this Bible study ministered to you the most and why? Write it out here.

_____
_____
_____
_____
_____
_____
_____
_____

Say Matthew 11:28-30 from memory. Have the person you say it to sign their name.

_____

Remember this Bible study is all about positioning yourself to be in an attitude of rest at the beginning of your day. On the next page you will write out your prayer. Look over all the lessons and determine which aspect of each lesson you want to use in your prayer. Your prayer should cover all of Matthew 11:28-30. I found that using the table of contents for the Bible study helps. Use the one I have included in this lesson as a guide; however you need to write your own. There is no wrong way.

Your Prayer:
_____
_____
_____
_____
_____
_____
_____
_____
_____
_____
_____
_____
_____
_____
_____
_____
_____
_____
_____
_____
_____
_____
_____
_____
_____
_____
_____
_____

Please keep in mind that God wants us to have fun and enjoy this life He has given us. Not everything is about work and service. Some days He simply tells me to do nothing or He tells me to have fun. He makes time for Nathan and I to go fishing. Jesus said in *John 10:10-*"*The thief cometh not, but for to steal, and to kill, and to destroy: I am come that they might have life, and that they might have it more **abundantly**.*"

Business can very well be a thief, but Jesus gives us life. Always working and never enjoying life is robbing yourself of the abundant life that Christ came to bring you. Be sensitive to His leading and He will make sure you have times of relaxation and fun! Live and walk in rest everyday; all for His glory and to honor all that Christ did to give you an abundant life!

Father I pray for each person that has completed this Bible study. I ask that You quicken them every day to come to You and that You reassure them of your Supremacy. Remind them continually how trustworthy You are and that You are truly faithful to Your own. Bless them as they come to You and give them courage to be real with You and themselves. Prove Yourself to them in a mighty way as they labor to enter that wonderful rest You have promised and speak to them throughout their day. Show them every area that they have not given You control, in the big ones and small ones. But most of all help us all to walk in this rest to bring You glory and Honor; to be a blessing to others and the Kingdom; to be a people that are mighty and strong and at peace. Blessings, Glory and Honor to You Jesus!!!

Kamikaze for Christ
Topical Bible Study
Walking in Rest
Dana Poole

Poolend1@gmail.com

281-650-9932

www.ingramcontent.com/pod-product-compliance
Lightning Source LLC
Chambersburg PA
CBHW060758090426
42736CB00002B/78